UFO photographed in Passaic, New Jersey, USA, July 1952; and close-up of the same UFO.

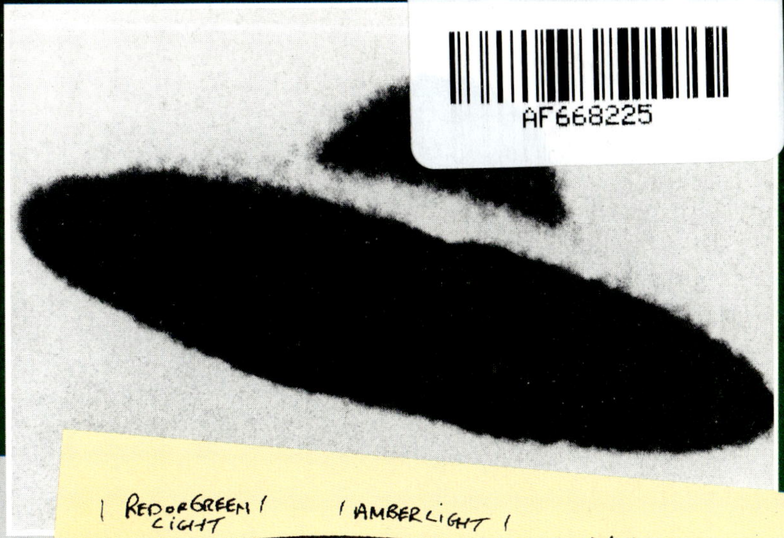

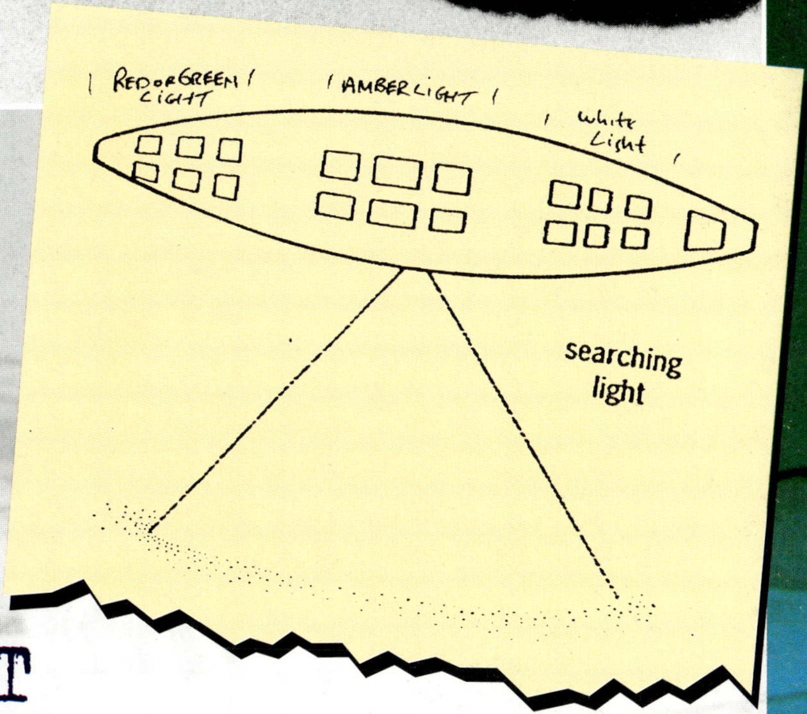

UFOs DO EXIST

UFO stands for *unidentified flying object*. A UFO is something moving in the sky that you cannot recognise as a star or planet, comet, meteor, airplane, helicopter, balloon, rocket, cloud or bird, etc. In other words a UFO is a strange object flying in the sky.

If you are watching the sky one night and you notice a star move, it may not be a shooting star. If it is not a satellilte or an airplane, it could be a UFO.

Although planes have white lights, they also have colored ones that flash brightly and sharply like strobe lights. Lights on UFO's are also white but they are much more powerful than those of an aircraft. You may notice that the colored lights on UFO's do not flash like aircraft lights. UFO's often have a number of these colored lights – not just the single red, green and white lights found on airplanes.

If you see a light in the sky suddenly change direction, it cannot be an airplane. Airplanes travel on straight or on smooth curved paths, while UFOs can suddenly dart up or down. You might be watching a helicopter, but be aware that UFOs are usually much quieter than helicopters.

Sometimes UFOs will shine brilliant searchlights onto the ground and light everything up as if it were day.

Above is the sketch Mrs Bette Jackson of Northfield, England, made after a zeppelin-shaped UFO bathed her house and yard with a great beam of light. The craft was light gray with square patches of red or green at one end, amber in the middle and white patches at the other end. It made a droning noise as it floated first to one side of the house and then to the other. Eventually the lights went out and the object disappeared. The whole sighting lasted nearly half an hour.

SCI-fact: UFOs can do things that no plane or jet could do.

WHAT SHAPE

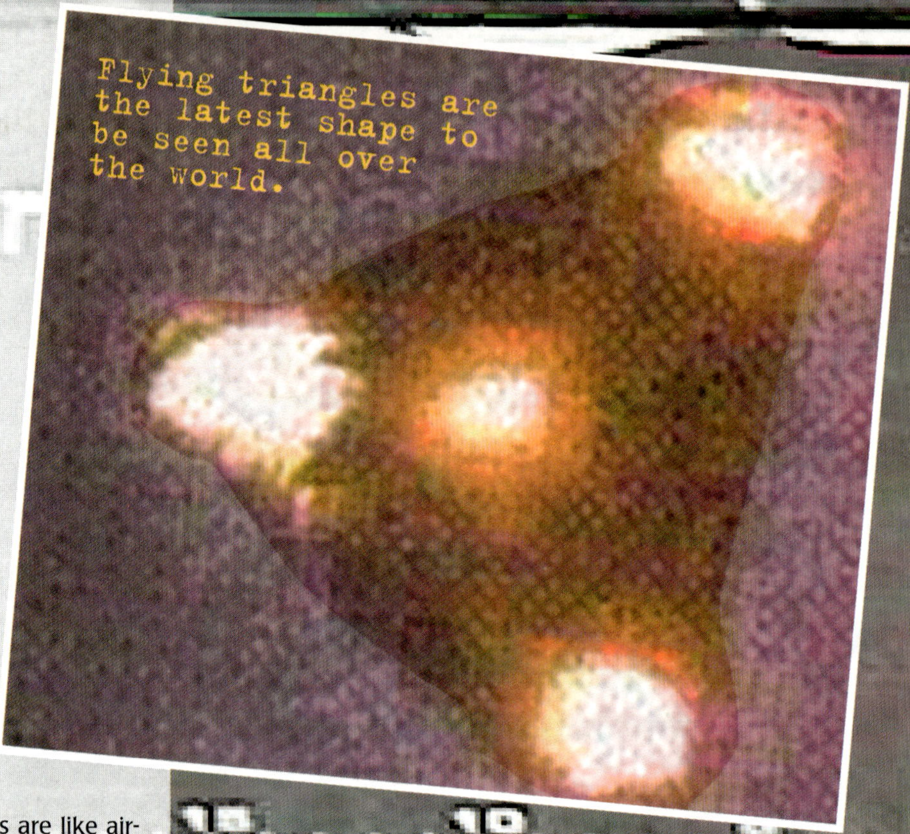

Flying triangles are the latest shape to be seen all over the world.

Most sightings are of flying disks that look like upside-down saucers with domes on the top. It is this kind of UFO that is known as a flying saucer.

Flying saucers are often quite small – no bigger than a small airplane – but monster discs as big if not bigger than very large water towers. The cigar-shaped crafts are sometimes as long as football fields. There are also triangle-shaped crafts that often have lights at the corners as well as along the sides. Many other shapes have been observed but the ones that are usually reported are disks, giant "cigars" and triangles.

Large UFOs that are shaped like giant cigars are like aircraft carriers. They carry the smaller disc-shaped UFOs and act as launching pads. Some people have seen flying saucers drop out of the open end of these big 'space-airships'. The little discs seem to fly away on a mission only to return to be reboarded by the mother craft when they have completed their task. These so-called mother craft may be 300 ft (100m) or more in length and often have patches of light along their sides.

Although some UFOs have been seen with wings and tails, they do not resemble airplanes.

Flying triangles, some of which are huge, are the latest shape to be seen all over the world. They often have lights on the corners and rows of lights down the sides.

On September 26, 1993 at 9.30 pm, a huge black flying triangle flew low over Bakewell, England. It performed several maneuvers over the town and was seen by numerous witnesses. A truck driver moving in the same direction as the flying triangle overtook it while travelling at a speed of 40mph (65km-h).

Do YOU believe in visitors from outer space?

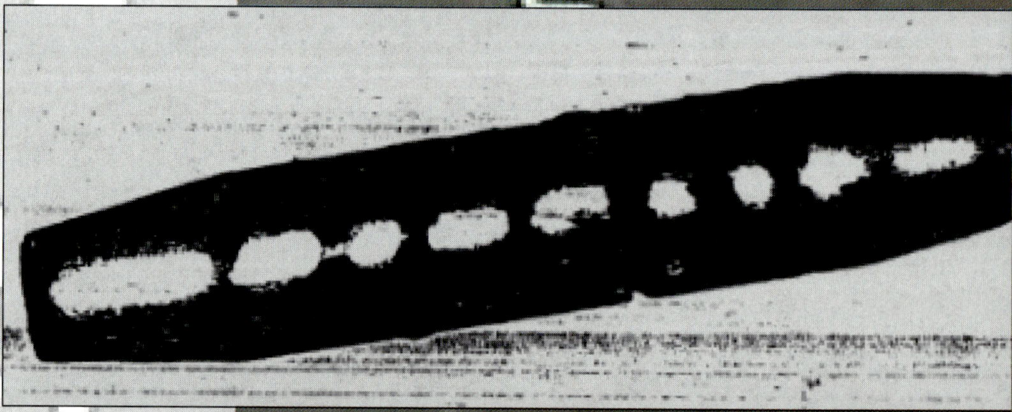

A cigar-shaped mother craft.

SCI-fact: The majority of flying saucers are small, the size of a small airplane...

EXAMINING THE EVIDENCE

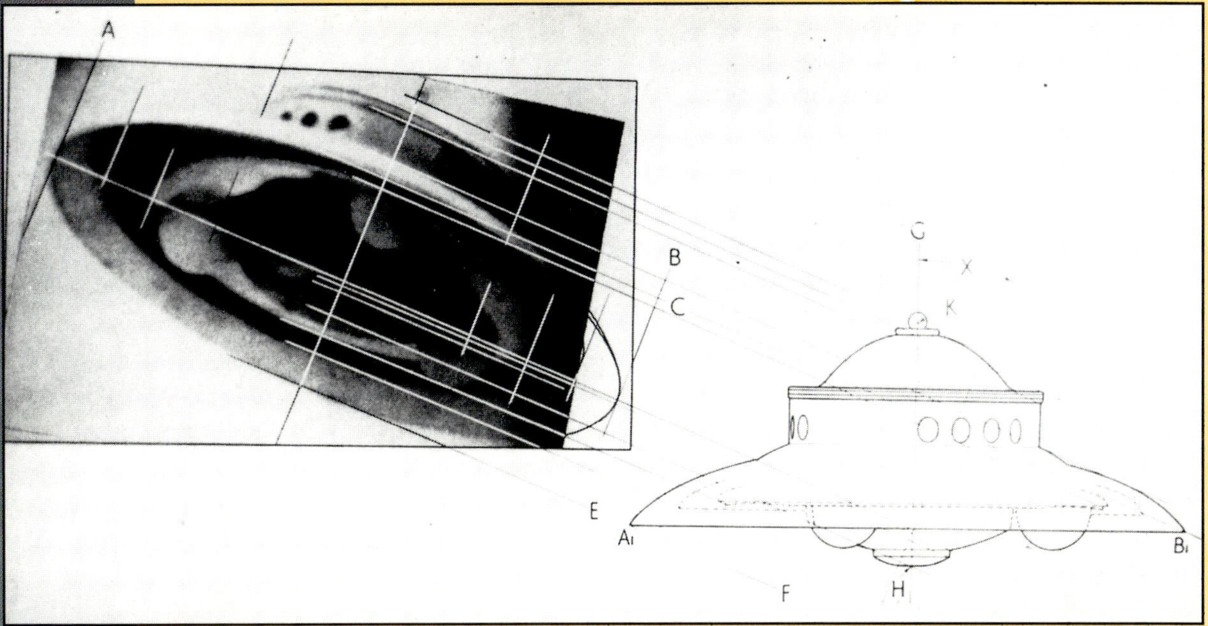

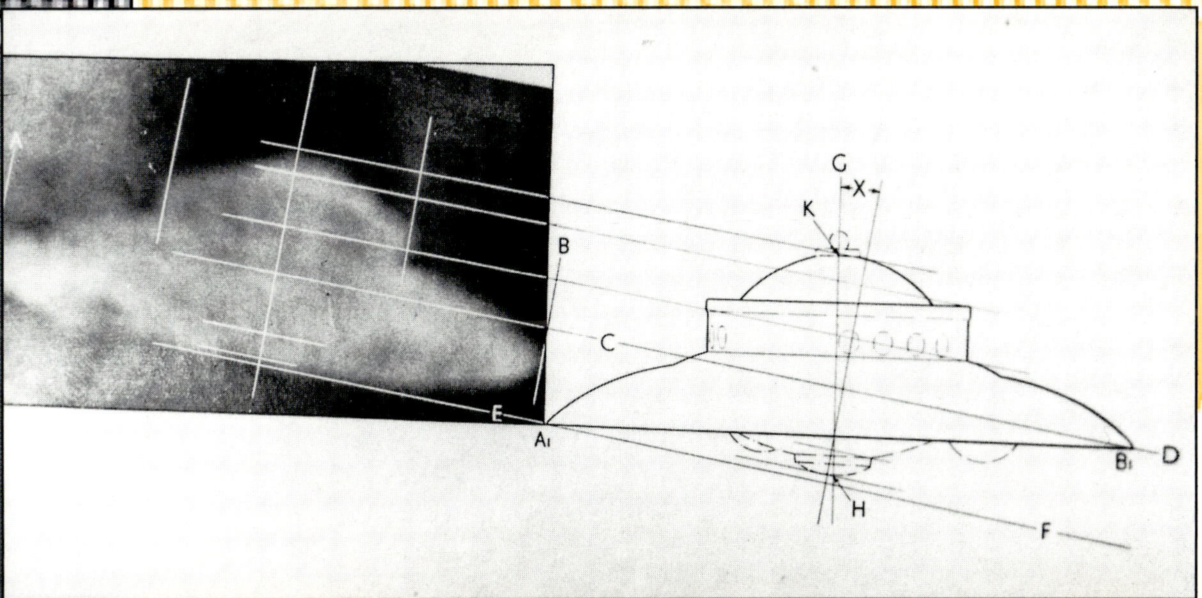

George Adamski took the pictures at the bottom of the opposite page and the one at the top of this page. Many people said they were too good to be true – that they had to be fakes. Yet a year later, Stephen Darbishire, took the lower picture in Lancashire, England which turned out to be exactly the same craft as the one in Adamski's pictures, proving they were not fakes. (From Space, Gravity and the Flying Saucer, by Leonard Cramp)

SCI-fact: ... mother craft can sometimes be as long as a football field.

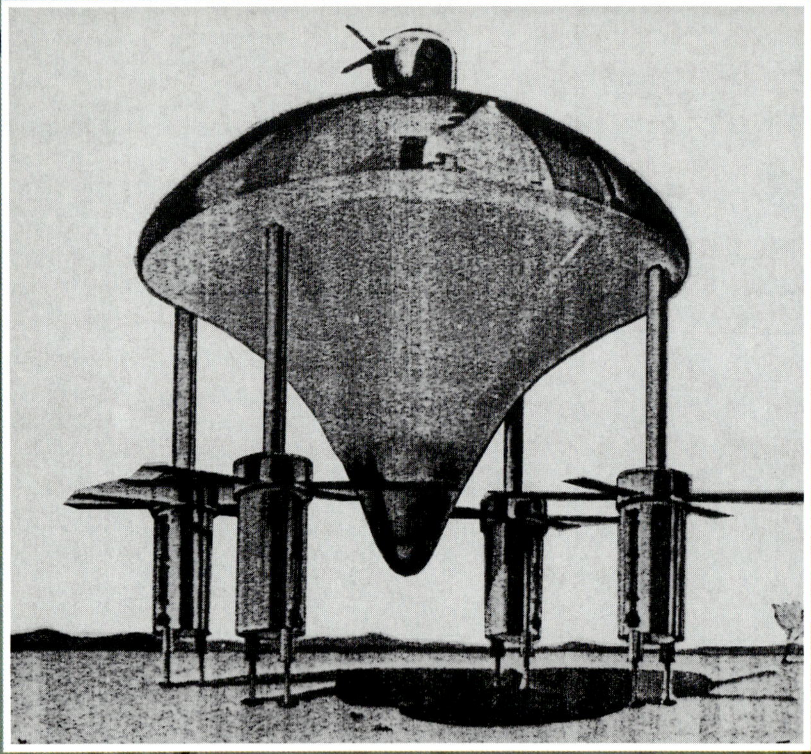

Drawing based on Ezekiel's description of the spacecraft that visited him and took him for flights. (after The Spaceships of Ezikiel by Joseph Blumrich)

A drawing published in 1909 of an 'aerial craft' observed over Peterborough, England, by a Police Officer Kettle - 'an absolutely trustworthy witness'

WHEN DID UFOs START?

UFOs are not new. As long as our records go back their existance has been noted. In the Bible there are references to events some people now imagine as possible UFO sightings.

The Book of Ezekiel in the *Old Testament* describes how the prophet may have been taken, on more than one occasion, from one place to another in what appears to have been a spacecraft. There are also accounts of fiery chariots and strange flying clouds in the Old Testament. A top NASA scientist sketched his vision of the craft that apparently visited the prophet Ezekiel (see above).

An aerial phenomenon was seen in Nuremberg, Germany, on April 14, 1561. When checking the ancient sketch pictured on the opposite page, you will note that the cylinders pictured in the drawing contain round objects; some of these objects appear to be landing in the lower right corner where you see the smoke rising (drawing from a collection at the Zurich Central Library).

Before large aircraft had been developed, giant space-airships visited many parts of the world. These were often observed in North America during and after 1896, as well as in parts of Europe including Peterborough in England.

Reports of strange sights in the skies continued through the first half of the Twentieth Century. It was American pilot Kenneth Arnold, however, who started the modern flying saucer scare. On June 24, 1947, while flying over the Cascade Mountains in search of a plane crash, Arnold saw a flight of disk-shaped objects travelling at over 1000 mph (1600km-h). He noted that they were, "skipping along like saucers" and the name *flying saucer* was born. Many people still call all UFOs *flying saucers* no matter what shape they may be.

Following this sighting, thousands of Americans saw strange craft in the sky and millions of sightings have taken place across the world. Because there are no earthly explanations for these events, many people feel that UFOs visit from beyond our planet.

SCI-fact: UFOs visited earth long before the discovery of aircraft ...

This illustration, taken from the Nuremberg Broadsheet, 1561, is of a very frightful spectacle seen in the sky over Nuremberg, Germany on April 14, 1561

KENNETH ARNOLD
JUNE 24, 1947

In broad daylight on June 24, 1947, Kenneth Arnold, an experienced mountain pilot and business man from Boise, Idaho, sighted nine wingless craft in the Cascade region of the Rocky Mountains. His eye was caught by a sudden glare of sunlight reflected off what appeared to be a highly polished surface. As his eyes focused on the source of the flash, he saw a rising, echelon formation of brilliant metallic objects in a chain five miles (8km) long. They flashed across his field of vision very quickly, but he was able to take a timing using his on-board instruments, estimating the speed of the nine anomalous forms at well over a 1000 mph (1600km-h). There were, of course, no aircraft at the time that could fly at speeds in excess of 700 mph (1100km-h) so, whatever they were, they were not conventional aircraft. Arnold noticed that the objects had no wings, were disk-shaped and "flew like saucers would if you skipped them across water." Kenneth Arnold, the first reliable witness and the one who sparked the use of the term flying saucer, was voluntarily searching for a lost plane at the time. He was experienced in mountain rescue work, and a deputy sheriff. You would, therefore, expect his eyesight to be first class, his reasoning to be sound, and his testimony to be utterly reliable. It is interesting to note that Arnolds clings to his story to this day.

In 1952 Kenneth Arnold published a book, *The Coming of the Saucers*, about his own and other UFO sightings – nearly five years after the big event.

Do YOU believe in visitors from outer space?

SCI-fact: Sightings of UFOs date back to biblical times . . .

UFOs OVER MEXICO

Ever since the eclipse of the sun on July 11, 1991, millions of people in Mexico have spotted UFOs in their skies. More than a thousand professional and home videos have recorded these events and Mexican TV has featured many hours of programs about the OVNIs, the Mexican name for UFOs. Most Mexicans accept these aerial visitors as possible friends.

Just after noon on July 11, 1991, millions of Mexicans were watching a very special eclipse of the sun. As they watched the sun disappearing, they saw a bright UFO appear. Many people unknown to one another caught this UFO on their home video cameras, so the vision must have been a real object, one that could easily be seen from many different places.

Since then the Mexican skies have never been free of UFOs. The reason many Mexicans readily accept their UFO visitors is because these visitations confirm the prophecies of their Mayan ancestors.

The Mayan priests said that there have been four suns or different ages of man. According to the priests we were in the fifth age but the eclipse of July 11, 1991, would begin the sixth age. This would lead to encounters with the "masters of the stars", thus heralding "coming earth changes".

The Mexicans took the vast number of UFO sightings that followed the eclipse to be a sign that the masters of the stars were visiting them. When their sacred volcano Popocatapetl, which had been sleeping, began to wake up and spurt smoke, they believed in the ancient Mayan prophecy even more.

If Popocatapetl fully erupts it will blanket Mexico City in ash and debris.

The visiting UFOs have shown great interest in the awakening volcano and some Mexicans hope the UFOs have come to quell the threatened eruption.

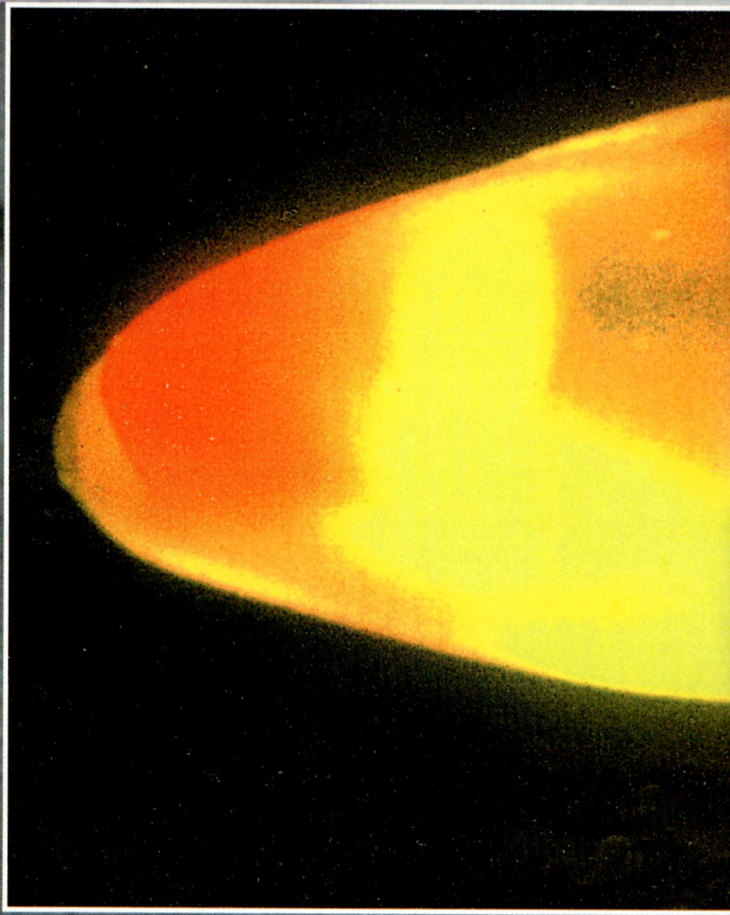

Many photographs and videos have been taken by Mexican people during, and since, an eclipse of the sun on 11 July, 1991.

The area between dotted lines shows path of eclipse & area of main UFO sightings.

UFO SCI-fact: Since 1991 millions of people in Mexico have seen UFOs...

Do YOU believe in visitors from outer space?

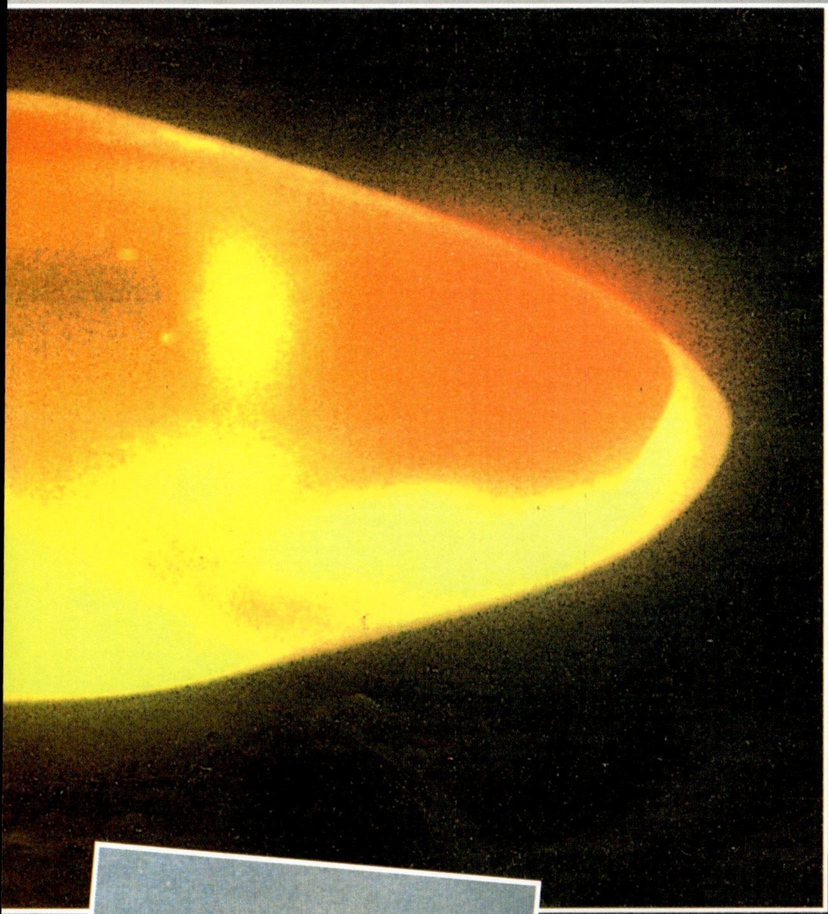

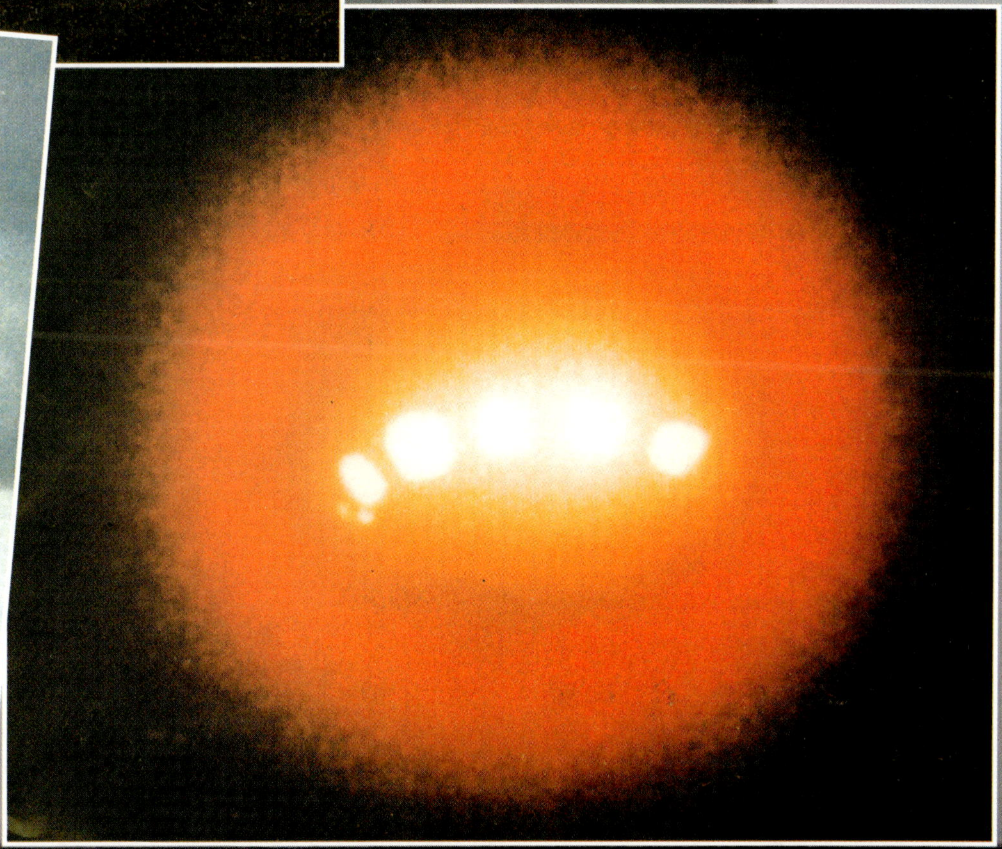

SCI-fact: ... more than a thousand professional and home videos have been made.

DO UFOs CRASH?

Millions of UFO sightings have occurred around the world. Rarely has there been a report of a UFO in trouble or actually crashing.

There have been a number of cases where things have been seen to fall from UFOs. These include metals and strange lumps of rock-like material or lava. Another odd material attributed to flying saucers is called 'angel hair' because it looks like long strands of cotton. Angel hair is usually observed as it is being sown by pairs of disks. Some of it has been studied in laboratories and one lab report said it resembled radioactive cotton.

There have been hundreds of sightings of angel hair but most were in the 1950s and 1960s, with very few sightings occurring in the past few years.

At about the same time as the crash known as *The Roswell Incident* (see page 13), 150 miles (250km) further west in New Mexico, a flying saucer was found by archaeologists who were working in the desert near the crash site. The craft was stuck in the side of a hill and several bodies of small human-like creatures were still in the machine or scattered on the ground outside. They resembled grays (see page 12) but had small eyes and only four fingers.

Not all the creatures were dead, however, and Grady Barnett and Gerald Anderson, who were there, say they were taken in great secrecy to military bases and that at least one survived for a year or more. Apparently autopsies were performed on the dead.

A great controversy surrounds this event because US authorities continue to say that nothing happened, whereas research conducted with friends of some of the people involved gives another story.

The books written about the Roswell Incident may be tough to read but it is important to read such books if you wish to make up your own mind. One of these books is called *Crash at Corona* by Stanton Friedman and Don Berliner.

There have been reports of other UFO crashes and they too have been hushed-up by the authorities. Not all these reports are from the United States. Reports have been filled from Britain, Russia and Scandinavia.

A college professor identified this cobweb-like material that fell from the sky over New York in 1955 as heavily damaged, radioactive fiber. But no one could say where it came from!

'Threads of the Virgin', resembling vaporized wool or nylon, was left by UFOs over Oloron and Gaillac in France October, 1952.

Angel hair, Ichinoseki City, Japan.

SCI-fact: Millions of sightings have occurred, with few signs of UFOs being in difficulty ...

AIRCRAFT AND UFOs

In May, 1948, the pilots of a flight of six Meteor jets saw a flying saucer that was 100 feet (30m) in diameter far above them. Two jets climbed up to take a closer look. They noticed a flat-bottomed disc with a dome on top and three hemispheres on the underside. Radar operators had the UFO on their screens. As the jets approached, the UFO shot straight up into the sky at the enormous speed of 15000 mph (24000km-h) and disappeared.

There are many cases of jets chasing UFOs and of UFO's being caught on radar. On the evening of January 6, 1995, a Boeing 737 jet liner was coming in to land at England's Ringway Airport when a wedge-shaped UFO, with many small lights and a stripe down its side, streaked past them. It so startled the pilots that they instinctively ducked as it went by.

A man driving past the airport at the time said it was a "a triangular aircraft darting about the sky. It was able to move sideways, right and left, and tilt over backwards, doing maneuvers no other aircraft could do."

UFO
SCI-file

ARE THERE BEINGS IN UFOs?

Entities – we cannot always call them people – have been seen many times outside UFOs that have landed. Sometimes they have been seen at the portholes of low-flying UFOs by aircraft pilots when the UFOs have fallen into formation with them. Occasionally extraterrestrials (ETs) are noticed working on hovering UFOs as was the case in Papua, New Guinea (see page 14).

'Human' ETs are beings from UFOs that look almost exactly like us. In a line up at a bus-stop you would not be able to tell them from humans. The Nordic type are over 6 feet (1.8m) tall, have blond hair and white, almost transparent skin.

'Grays' resembling the ones above, or like the mask on page 21, are small – less than 5 feet (1.5m) – have gray skin, very large heads compared to their bodies, enormous almond-shaped eyes and holes for ears and noses. Sometimes they have webbed feet and three or four fingers which may also be webbed like those of a frog. Described by the more human-looking ETs as soldiers, they may be manufactured by genetic engineering.

There are many references to ETs that look like the fairies, gnomes and trolls found in story books. Some people think the fairy stories from long ago describe little people who came from UFOs. People in those days were nor familiar with spaceships and they imagined that these creatures came from a place called Fairyland.

Some ETs are said to resemble large, hairy ape-men. They may be as much as 8 feet (2.5m) tall and may have glowing eyes or make weird wailing noises.

One kind of being from UFOs has been described as a lizard-man with green skin and reptile-like eyes. In one reported case a lizard-man was accompanied by a hairy ape-man and two silver-suited human-like ETs. They came from an almost invisible, cone-shaped object that hovered close by. A cow near the ETs floated off the ground and up into their UFO, which then took off.

In 1973 there was an invasion of UFOs in Quebec, Canada. The strange fire-creature in the drawing (center) above was seen in the early morning of November 22 by a lady in a house in Joliette, Quebec. The being was about 4 feet (1.2m) tall with round glowing eyes that were three times the size of human eyes. The head was surrounded by a glowing, flaming light pattern. The lady did not feel at all frightened by the apparition but her dog and cat were terrified. There had been UFO sightings in the Joliette area for several weeks so although she did not see a UFO near by, she assumed that there must have been one.

Do YOU believe in visitors from outer space?

Major Jesse Marcel, intelligence officer at the Roswell military base in July, 1947, holds the tattered remains of a flying disk found on a nearby sheep ranch. Marcel maintained that "the material seemed not of this Earth."

Roswell Daily Record

RAAF Captures Flying Saucer On Ranch in Roswell Region

Claims Army Is Stacking Courts Martial

House Passes Tax Slash by Large Margin

Security Council Paves Way to Talks On Arms Reductions

No Details of Flying Disk Are Revealed

Ex-King Carol Weds Mme. Lupescu

Miners and Operators Sign Highest Wage Pact in Histor

Some of Soviet Satellites May Attend Paris Meeting

Roswellians Have Differing Opinions On Flying Saucers

American League Wins All-Star Game

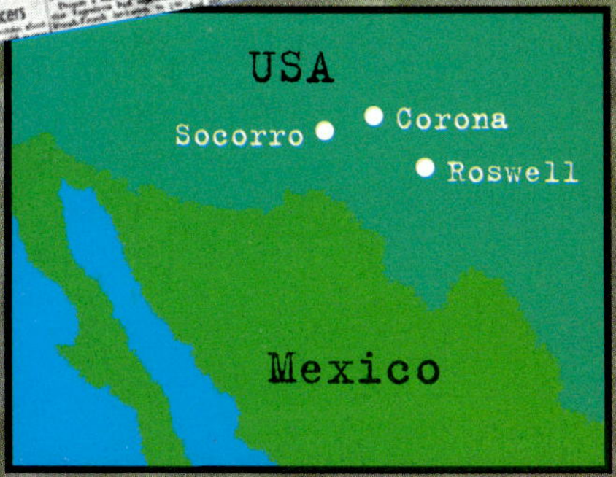

THE ROSWELL INCIDENT

On Thursday, July 3, 1947, William Brazel, a rancher, was searching around the Foster Ranch at a place called Corona with the help of Dee Proctor, the seven-year-old daughter of his neighbour. There had been a gigantic thunderstorm the night before and they were looking to see what damage had been done. It was then that they found a field full of mysterious-looking strips of metal and what looked like bits of wood. The metal was very thin but could not be crumpled or damaged in any way by hammers or blow-torches, and some of the wood had strange markings – a bit like Egyptian hieroglyphics. The men from the local airbase (Roswell) gathered up this material and issued a statement that the remains of a flying disk had been found at the ranch. Almost immediately the authorities withdrew this statement, saying that the pieces they had recovered were the remains of a weather balloon.

TOP SECRET

SCI-fact: ... in a number of cases metals or lava-like rocks have fallen from UFOs.

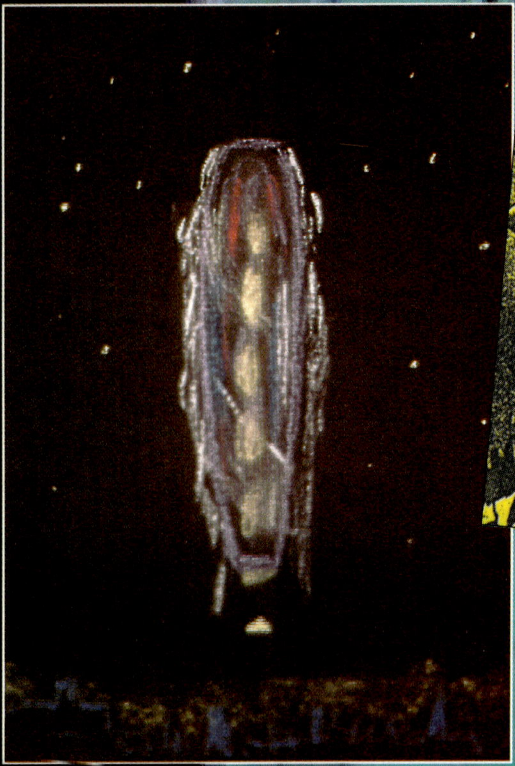

The illustration above depicts a UFO and its occupants over Papua New Guinea. At left is a giant cigar-shaped craft that was seen above Warminster, a small town in England that was subjected to many UFO visits in the 1960s.

FAMOUS UFO PLACES

Out of thousands of UFO reports, it is difficult to pick the most famous.

WARMINSTER

In this small town in England you have a better chance of seeing a UFO than almost anywhere else in Britain. To the north of the town is Cradle Hill where UFO buffs have skywatches that are often rewarded by the appearance of UFOs. This is because Cradle Hill is what is called a Ufocal. Ufocals are places that produce many UFO sightings. However, the whole area around Warminster has had more than its fair share of attention from UFOs.

It all began on Christmas morning, 1964. UFOs flew over the town and bombarded people and houses with savage sound waves. As strange happenings continued through 1965, the local people began to think that one thing might be causing all the trouble, so that's what they called the phenomena – the thing. The sound waves killed a flock of pigeons in flight and were blamed for the death of other creatures. The UFOs that produced the awful sounds apparently came from cigar-shaped craft that sometimes hovered in the skies. For 30 minutes, one hung motionless in the sky and was described as looking like the sketch above (left).

Another of these giant cigars, with side windows that glowed with a yellow light, was observed just 16 days later. This kind of UFO had been photographed by George Adamski 12 years earlier (see page 4).

If you want to know more about what went on in Warminster during 1965 read *The Warminster Mystery* by Arthur Shuttlewood. This book also reports the strange phone calls that were made to Arthur Shuttlewood by some UFO-nauts who said they came from a planet called Aenstria.

SCI-fact: There have been many famous UFO places around the world, we are still receiving information ...

Mother ship, Canary Islands.

One of the imprints left at Soccorro by the saucer.

PAPUA NEW GUINEA

Papua, New Guinea is part of a large island north of Australia. In 1959 its inhabitants were treated to several months of UFO sightings. On June 27 at 6.45 p.m., missionaries at a tiny outpost spotted a large, bright object low in the sky. By then the sun had set and the missionaries and native people were able to see that the craft was like a circular platform with a transparent dome on top.

That was not the most amazing thing, however, for they could see four human-like figures silhouetted against the craft. These figures seemed to be working around the deck of the UFO and would occasionally disappear and reappear. Everyone who could was watching this event in the partly cloudy skies, including Reverend William Gill, who was head of the mission.

The next night the UFO came back closer then ever. Reverend Gill and others waved to the UFO-nauts and they waved back. When a flashlight was directed at it, the craft rocked back and forth in acknowledgement. The whole mission waved their arms and flashed their lights as the craft came nearer. On the first night UFOs were seen for nearly five hours but on the second night the sightings started at 6 p.m. and was over in less than two hours.

SOCORRO, NEW MEXICO

Lonnie Zamora was a policeman who, on the afternoon of April 24, 1964, noticed a UFO descending close by. It was, he said, emitting a flame. It proved to be an egg-shaped craft resting on metal legs. Near it were two white-cloaked figures. The craft made loud sounds and streaked away, disappearing from sight. The craft left indentations on the ground where it had rested and plants in the area were still smouldering when Zamora and fellow officer arrived. You can read all about this case in *Socorro Saucer - The closest encounter of them all* by Ray Stanford. Similar egg-shaped craft and occupants have been seen in France, Belgium, Germany, Italy, Brazil, Australia and Canada as well as in the United States.

SCI-fact: ... mis-information as well as genuine information has been leaked by the authorities about events such as Roswell.

George Adamski

Adamski wanted the visitor to have a souvenir so he gave him a photographic plate from his telescope's camera that just happened to be in his pocket. The photo (see page 5) was taken when a UFO, maybe the same one, returned the plate. When it was developed, a lens-shaped device together with a type of strange writing appeared on the plate.

This time Adamski's evidence was corroborated by a well-known explorer, Marcel Homet, in a book about his explorations in South America called *Sons of the Sun*. Homet found the symbols that appear in Adamski's picture on rocks in Amazonia. You will notice that some of the symbols are exactly the same.

During the Second World War, a French priest claimed he was taken in a UFO to a planet called Båavi, a planet of the constellation of the Centaur, which contains some of our nearest stars. He certainly disappeared for a month and his relatives thought he was dead. When he came back he had more knowledge than one person could acquire in a lifetime of study. He also drew a technical sketch (see below right) of the craft which he called a "vaïdorge". You will see how similar the vaïdorge sketch is to those of Adamski and Homet.

Many people these days claim they have been placed under a form of hypnosis and floated into UFOs. While there, they have been subjected to medical examinations. We refer to these people as abductees.

CONTACTEES

Contactees are people who claim to have met and spoken with beings from flying saucers (we call them UFO-nauts in the same way that we call our spacemen astronauts).

We have already seen how one of George Adamski's pictures (see page 5) was corroborated by a schoolboy's photograph. Adamski went to a remote spot in the desert with four friends hoping to see a UFO and meet its occupants. While he was there a flying saucer landed close by and a UFO-naut conversed with him. One of his companions drew the UFO-naut (see drawing opposite) and showed him to be human-like, but much better looking than most humans.

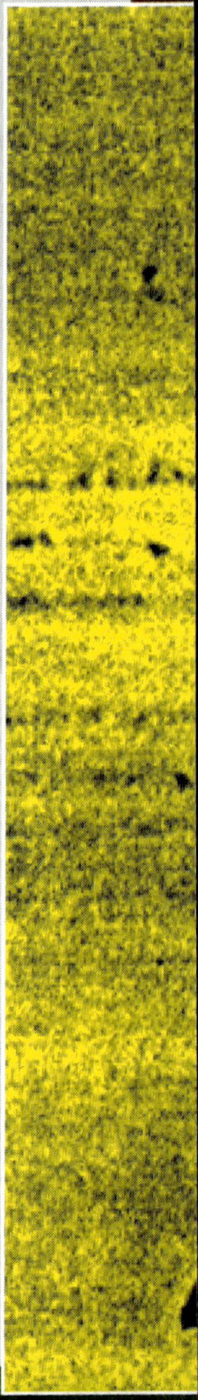

This cross section of a vaïdorge (right) looks like the similar ones above.

Far right: Writing from the Planet Bâavi.

UFO SCI-fact: Many people have described talking with ET's from UFOs or even being taken for rides aboard UFOs.

Do YOU believe in visitors from outer space?

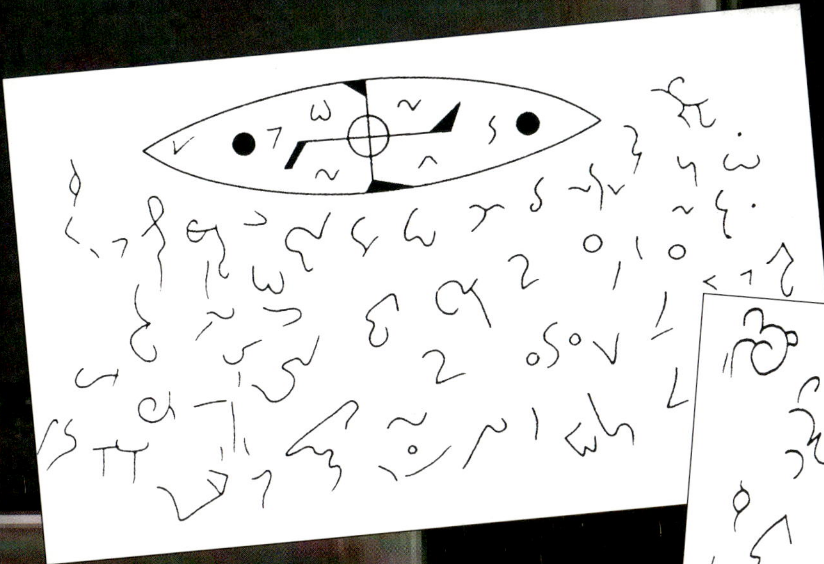

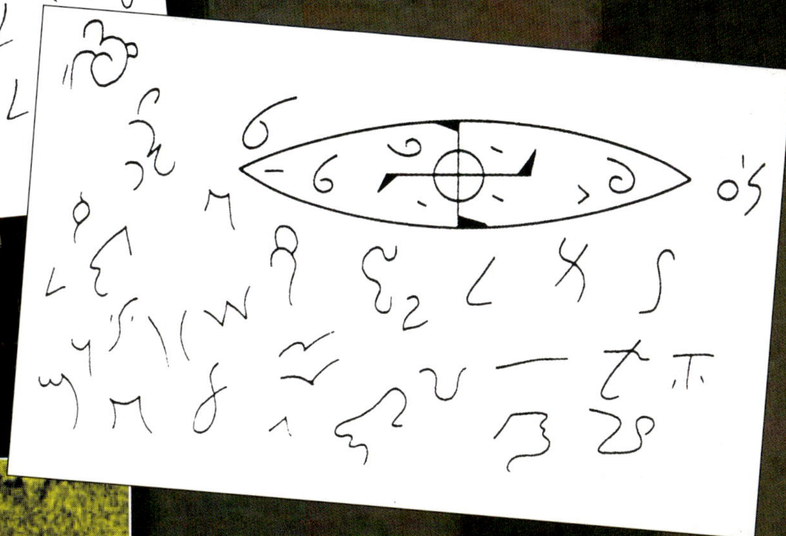

There is an uncanny similarity between these two pictures: one is from the Amazon while the other could be from much further afield!

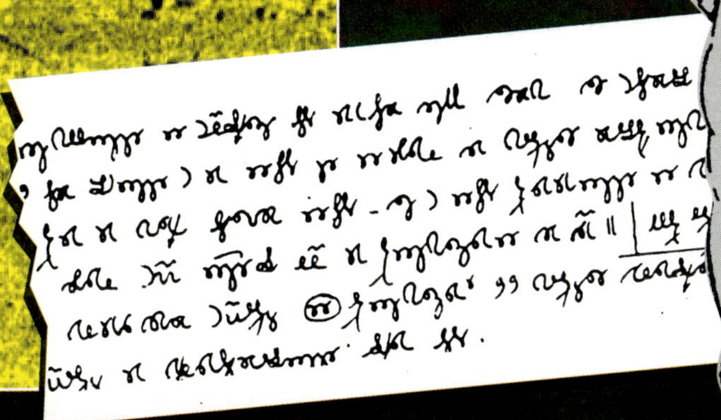

Alice Wells, who was there, drew this sketch of the UFO-naut that Adamski met.

SCI-fact: It seems that many UFOs are highly advanced inter-stellar vehicles.

WHAT IF I SEE A UFO?

Two boys hold a sketch of a black triangular craft they saw at Butleigh, England.

If you see a UFO on the ground close by, do not go near it. UFOs have strong force-fields around them and you could get hurt. UFOs usually try to avoid people. They seem to prefer the darkness and the countryside to being seen over cities in daylight.

Sometimes UFOs seem to want you to notice them – maybe even take photographs of them. This happened to a 15-year-old schoolboy I knew named Alex. He was out photographing his friends with his new camera when a group of UFOs appeared in the sky. He took the top picture on the opposite page.

At about the same time, Stephen Pratt, who was about the same age, took a picture that looked much like Alex's. Strangely, Stephen saw one UFO but three appeared in his photo (see page 19).

People who are exposed to UFOs close-up often complain that their skin feels as if it has been sunburned and that they developed headaches. Sometimes they are knocked out by the encounter and regain consciousness much later. In these cases the UFO usually projects a beam of light at the forehead of the person involved.

It is very likely that a local UFO study group will be very excited to have an account of your sighting. Some of the things they hope you will be able to tell them include the exact shape of the craft, the specific location of the lights you observed, its speed and especially whether it made any maneuvers that indicated it could not be an airplane.

You can get an idea of how large UFOs are by holding your outstretched hand at arms length and judging how many fingers the craft spans. (Of course, if it is very small this method won't work.)

If you have a camera or your family has a camcorder, try to get your sighting on film. Although taking a good picture of a UFO is very difficult, your photograph just might be the UFO picture of the year!

It is also useful to know how long the UFO was in sight, and if it took off like a speeding plane or just suddenly disappeared from sight. Any noises it made should be noted as well.

Children often get better sightings than adults. Not long ago a boy knocked at my door to show me a sketch he'd made of a triangular UFO that had hovered over his house at a very low level. This boy lived behind my house yet I had not seen or heard anything unusual.

The two boys in the picture above were in Somerset, England, in August 1995, when a triangular, jumbo-jet-sized UFO flew close to the car in which they were riding. It was moving slowly and silently and had a pulsating red light on each corner. It suddenly flew straight up and disappeared. The boys drew a sketch of the craft they had seen.

Like the boys in the picture, immediately draw what you have seen before your memory fades.

SCI-fact: If you see a UFO do not go near it ...

Do YOU believe in visitors from outer space?

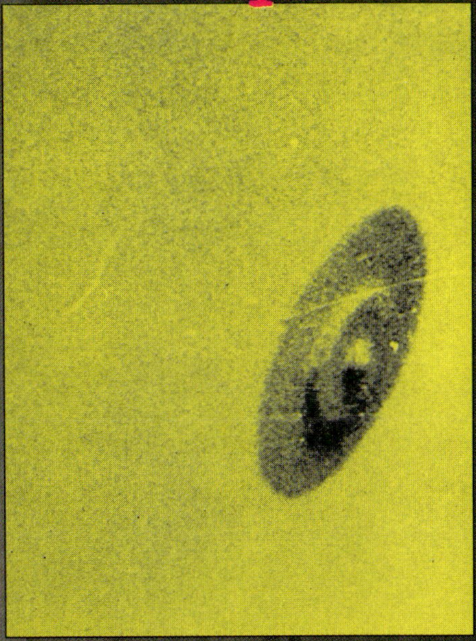

Above: The picture Alex Birch took in June, 1962, at Mosborough, England.

Right: A picture, similar to Alex Birch's, taken by Stephen Pratt in March, 1966, at Conisborough, England.

Many people say they do not believe in UFOs because they have never seen one. Ask them how often they look at the sky and they may suddenly realize that they have missed seeing UFOs because they are always looking at the ground.

SCI-fact: ... these craft have strong fields around them and you could get hurt.

CHILDREN & UFOs

In several places in this book, I have mentioned sightings made by children. In fact, it sometimes seems that UFOs prefer to appear to children instead of to adults.

It is not often you can see a UFO and its occupants on your way to school but that is what happened to the children at an elementary School near Pembroke in Wales. During the afternoon of Friday, February 4, 1977, some children noticed a silvery metallic object on the ground with a silver-suited figure standing nearby not far from the school. Fourteen children saw the UFO and its occupant and some drew sketches. They all agreed that the craft was saucer-shaped with a dome on top and that the UFO-naut wore a helmet or had big ears.

Sightings in Wales were common at this time: children at a school not far from the one previously mentioned saw a silver-white cigar-shaped UFO three days later and a similar craft was seen at another school in Wales about one week later.

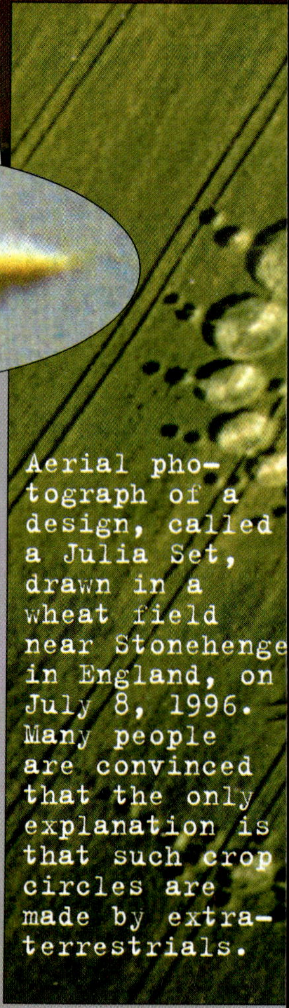

Aerial photograph of a design, called a Julia Set, drawn in a wheat field near Stonehenge in England, on July 8, 1996. Many people are convinced that the only explanation is that such crop circles are made by extra-terrestrials.

This is just a small selection of the drawings made by children at Broad Haven Primary School after a UFO landed near their school.

UFO SCI-fact: UFOs seem to like appearing to children

CONCLUSION

ON BEING A SCEPTIC

When you read the newspapers you will often find controversy over UFOs. They will place the reports from people who have seen UFOs next to the opinions of someone who calls him or herself a sceptic. Unfortunately you often find that the sceptics have never read the evidence and they did not see what the person who made the report saw. Such people are unthinking sceptics. You should also be a sceptic and not believe everything you read or see about UFOs but you should be an honest, thinking sceptic who does not believe or disbelieve until they have read the evidence. It is often much easier to accept someone else's conclusion than to think for yourself. I am looking at a newspaper this minute that contains a double-page spread headed "The UneXplained" (the X is large because of the TV series "The X-Files") where, amongst several pictures of mysterious things like the Loch Ness Monster, there is a photo of the saucer that George Adamski photographed (page 5). Here's what a sceptic Mike Dash says: "It's almost certainly a chicken brooder or cut-down pith helmet with a couple of ping-pong balls stuck on the bottom. It's a fake and not a very good one at that."

What do YOU think?

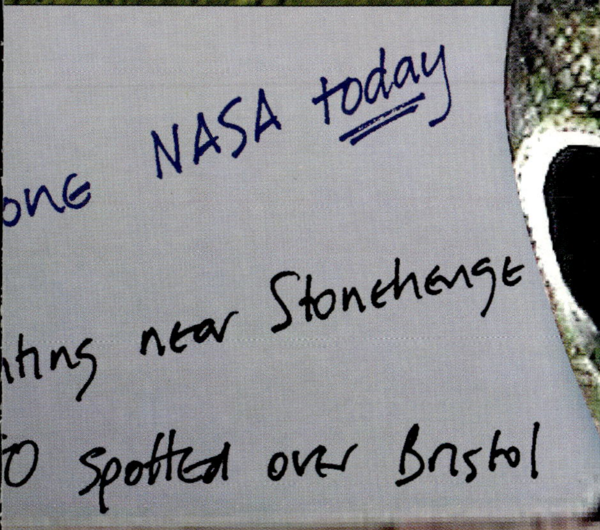

NOW Do YOU believe in visitors from outer space?

SCI-fact: Crop designs are too big and complicated to be the work of hoaxers

Do YOU believe in visitors from outer space?

In UFO Sci-file you'll find out all about Unidentified Flying Objects...

What do they look like?

Where could they come from?

Who has seen them?

How fast do they travel?

What do they do?

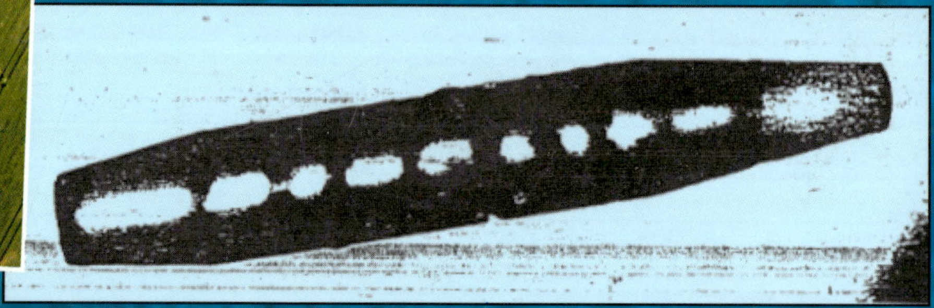

Written by Alan Watts
Designed by John Starke
Developed by Martin Rhodes-Schofield
Picture Library: Fortean

This edition published by Scholastic India Pvt. Ltd., 2014
Printed at Batra Art Press, New Delhi

6991

Activity ₹195
ISBN 978-93-5103-248-9
9 789351 032489
SCHOLASTIC
www.scholastic.co.in